On Deck

USS ALABAMA

By Al Adcock
Color by Don Greer
Illustrated by Richard Hudson

On Deck Number 1
squadron/signal publications

Introduction

The USS *AlLABAMA* (BB-60) was the fourth US naval vessel to bear the name of the great state of Alabama. The first *AlLABAMA* was a steam-powered, sidewheel coastal transport that was acquired in 1849. She was found to be unsuitable for naval service and was soon stricken from the naval list. The second USS *ALABAMA* served during the American Civil War from 1861 to 1865. This USS *ALABAMA* was also a steam-powered side-wheeler and she served with the US Federal Navy's Atlantic Blockade Squadron.

The Confederate States Navy also possessed a vessel named *AlLABAMA*. This ship was originally named the *ENRICA*, but was armed and commissioned into the CS Navy as the CSS *ALABAMA* in 1862. The CSS *ALABAMA* was utilized in the commerce raiding role in the eastern Atlantic, preying on Federal ships plying the trade routes between the United States and Europe. The CSS *ALABAMA* was finally caught and sunk off the coast of France by the Federal cruiser USS *KEARSARGE* in 1864.

The third USS *ALABAMA* (BB-8), commissioned in 1900, was one of the 16 US Navy battleships of President Theodore Roosevelt's 'Great White Fleet'. The Great White Fleet was sent around the world by President Roosevelt in order "to show the flag." During World War One the old USS *ALABAMA*, no longer a viable warship when compared to the newer dreadnought battleships of the British and German Navies, served as a gunnery training ship. The elderly battleship was decommissioned and scrapped following the war.

In 1939 Congress authorized the construction of four new battleships designated the *SOUTH DAKOTA* class. The new ships were named the *SOUTH DAKOTA* (BB-57), *INDIANA* (BB-58), *MASSACHUSETTS* (BB-59), and *ALABAMA* (BB-60). The *ALABAMA* was laid down at Norfolk Navy Yard, Portsmouth, Virginia on 1 February 1940. After two years of construction the *ALABAMA* was launched on 16 February 1942. Following her fitting out, the *ALABAMA* was commissioned on 16 August 1942 and began her shakedown cruise and underway training. The *ALABAMA* joined the US Atlantic fleet and Task Force 22 which was formed around the carrier USS *RANGER* (CV-4) escorting convoys. In May of 1943 the *ALABAMA* joined the Royal Navy escorting convoys in concert with the British Home Fleet.

On 1 August 1943 the *ALABAMA* and her sister ship, the *SOUTH DAKOTA*, sailed to Norfolk, Virginia for provisions, fuel, and a new captain and crew in preparation for sailing through the Panama Canal and into the Pacific Ocean and a different war. It would be 20 years until the *ALABAMA* would sail back through the 'big ditch' on her way to her final resting place. During her two years in the Pacific Theater in World War II, the *ALABAMA* fought from the Gilbert Islands in the central Pacific to Tokyo Bay, Japan.

Following World War II the USS *ALABAMA* was decommissioned and placed in reserve at Bremerton Navy Yard in Washington. On 1 June 1962 the *ALABAMA* was stricken from the US Navy list of ships and put up for scrapping. A group of concerned Alabama citizens, hearing of the plan to scrap the battleship, contacted the US Navy about preserving the gallant battleship as a war memorial. A total of one million US dollars was raised, largely by Alabama school children, to tow the *ALABAMA* back through the Panama Canal and construct a memorial park.

Today, the USS *ALABAMA* can be viewed and toured at the memorial located at Battleship Park on Mobile Bay, Mobile, Alabama. The display also includes a Vought-Sikorsky OS2U Kingfisher scout-observation aircraft — carried by the battleship from 1942 through 1945 — as well as many other historic aircraft.

(Previous Page) The USS *ALABAMA* (BB-60) was painted in Measure 12 camouflage during her Atlantic shakedown cruise in late 1942. The scheme was painted out before the *ALABAMA* departed for the Pacific in 1943. (US Navy)

ISBN 0-89747-399-X

If you have any photographs of aircraft, armor, soldiers or ships of any nation, particularly wartime snapshots, why not share them with us and help make Squadron/Signal's books all the more interesting and complete in the future. Any photograph sent to us will be copied and the original returned. The donor will be fully credited for any photos used. Please send them to:

Squadron/Signal Publications, Inc.
1115 Crowley Drive
Carrollton, TX 75011-5010

Если у вас есть фотографии самолётов, вооружения, солдат или кораблей любой страны, особенно, снимки времён войны, поделитесь с нами и помогите сделать новые книги издательства Эскадрон/Сигнал ещё интереснее. Мы переснимем ваши фотографии и вернём оригиналы. Имена приславших снимки будут сопровождать все опубликованные фотографии. Пожалуйста, присылайте фотографии по адресу:

Squadron/Signal Publications, Inc.
1115 Crowley Drive
Carrollton, TX 75011-5010

軍用機、装甲車両、兵士、軍艦などの写真を所持しておられる方はいらっしゃいませんか？どの国のものでも結構です。作戦中に撮影されたものが特に良いのです。Squadron/Signal社の出版する刊行物において、このような写真は内容を一層充実し、興味深くすることができます。当方にお送り頂いた写真は、複写の後お返しいたします。出版物中に写真を使用した場合は、必ず提供者のお名前を明記させて頂きます。お写真は下記にご送付ください。

Squadron/Signal Publications, Inc.
1115 Crowley Drive
Carrollton, TX 75011-5010

(Front Cover) The *Alabama*, in concert with other units of the US Third Fleet, uses her 16-inch guns to pound the Kamaishi Iron and Steel Works on the Japanese main island of Honshu on 14 July 1945.

Acknowledgements

US Navy	Battleship ALABAMA Memorial	Alice Hanes	Bill Parsons
Elsilrac	Carol Adcock	Barbara S. Kruse	Thad Rudd
Floating Drydock	Bill Tunnel	LTV Corporation	Walter Turner
National Archives	Real War Photos	EDO Corporation	
Dale Cavin	The Hook	Doug Siegfried	
Portsmouth Navy Shipyard, Virginia			

(Back Cover) The *ALABAMA* sends up a curtain of anti-aircraft fire to ward off Japanese air attacks during the campaign in the central Pacific during the late winter and spring of 1944.

(Above) The CSS *ALABAMA* was a steam-powered commerce raider used by the Navy of The Confederate States of America. The *ALABAMA* was built in England by the Laird Shipyard and commissioned in August of 1862. The *ALABAMA* wreaked havoc among the Federal fishing and merchant fleets before she was sunk by the USS *KEARSARGE* off the coast of France in 1864. (National Archives)

(Below) The USS *ALABAMA* (BB-8) was commissioned in 1900 and joined President Theodore Roosevelt's 'Great White Fleet' — so named because the ships' hulls were painted overall white. The Great White Fleet was sent around the world in 1907 "to show the flag". The obsolete *ALABAMA* served as a gunnery training ship in WW I and was decommissioned in 1920. (US Navy)

(Above) The USS *ALABAMA* (SSBN-731) is by far the most powerful of all of the vessels that have been named 'ALABAMA'. The nuclear powered submarine carries 24 Trident surface-to-surface ballistic missiles, each armed with several nuclear warheads. The *ALABAMA* was built by the Electric Boat Company and serves in the US Pacific Fleet. (US Navy)

3

The USS *ALABAMA* underwent sea trials in the Atlantic during 1942 wearing a Measure 12 camouflage scheme with an Ocean Gray base and irregular patches of Navy Blue. Vought OS2U Kingfisher floatplanes are spotted on the after deck and catapult. (Elsilrac)

The *ALABAMA* was moored at her present berth at Battleship Memorial Park, Mobile, Alabama in 1970. The battleship was painted in a Measure 27 scheme (overall Haze Gray) — the current standard paint scheme of the US Navy. (Elsilrac)

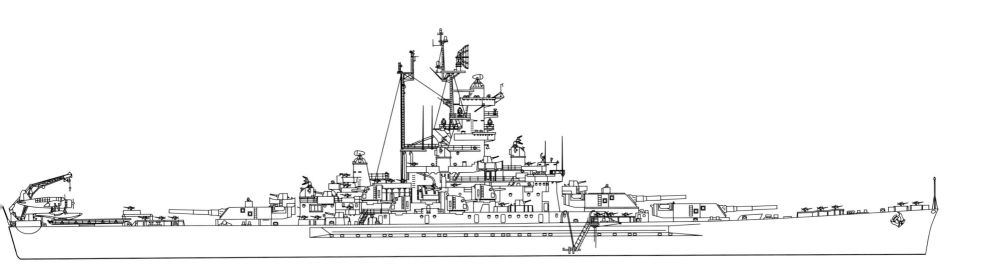

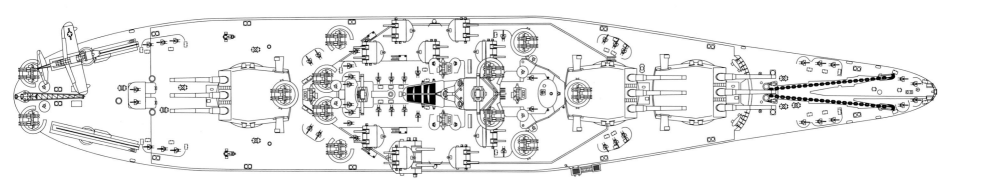

USS ALABAMA (BB-60)

Length:..........................679 Feet, 5 Inches
Beam:............................108 Feet, 1 Inch
Draught:........................36 Feet
Displacement:................44,800 Tons
Maximum Speed:.........28 Knots
Range:...........................16,000 Miles @ 15 Knots

Armament
9 x 16 Inch/45 Caliber Mk 6 Guns in Three Turrets
20 x 5 Inch/38 Caliber Mk 12 Guns in Ten Turrets
48 x 40mm AA Weapons in 12 Quad Mounts
56 x 20mm AA Weapons in Single/Dual Mounts
Machinery: 8 x Foster-Wheeler Oil Fired Boilers and 4 x
Westinghouse Turbines

(Right) Mrs. Lister Hill christens the battleship USS *ALABAMA* (BB 60) at Norfolk Navy Yard on 16 February 1942. After the launching, the ship was moved to a 'fitting out' dock where the remainder of her equipment, including guns, were installed. Despite the festivities, the first four months of 1942 were dark days for the Allies. The Japanese were on the rampage in the Pacific, Rommel's Afrika Korps was surging towards Egypt and the Suez Canal, and the Wehrmacht was pushing to the gates of Moscow and Leningrad. (Elsilrac)

US Navy Ship Designators

CV............ Fleet Aircraft Carrier
CVL......... Light Aircraft Carrier
BB.............Battleship
CA.............Heavy Cruiser
CL.............Light Cruiser
DD.............Destroyer
DE.............Destroyer Escort

(Below) The *ALABAMA* was launched into the James River in Virginia on 16 February 1942 and then towed to a fitting out dock to receive her government furnished equipment, or GFE. GFE included her 16-inch guns and turrets, five inch guns, anti-aircraft weapons, radars, and communications equipment. Thousands of man hours were still needed to get her ready to fight the Axis. (Elsilrac)

(Above and Below) The *ALABAMA*, moored at her berth in Mobile Bay, Alabama in 1996, is now painted in a modified Measure 22 camouflage scheme — a Navy Blue and Haze Gray scheme similar to the one she wore in 1943 while escorting convoys in the North Atlantic. The hull number on the bow is oversized at the discretion of the USS *ALABAMA* Battleship Commission. (Carol Adcock)

The bow contains the anchors, one port (left side) and one starboard (right side), the jack staff, and deck mounted 20mm anti-aircraft guns. Draught markings are painted just behind the stem — the sharply edged part of the bow that cuts through the water. (Author)

The hull side contains the internal 12.2-inch thick main armor belt. The armor belt is angled at 19 degrees to better deflect incoming enemy fire. Over thirty-nine percent, some 15,000 tons, of the *ALABAMA*'s displacement is devoted to armor protection. (Author)

The port side anchor is secured in the hawsepipe. An adapter collar keeps the anchor from scrubbing and damaging the hull. (Author)

The fantail is fitted with an aircraft handling crane and a pair of quad 40mm anti-aicraft guns. An oversize hull number is also painted on the stern. (Author)

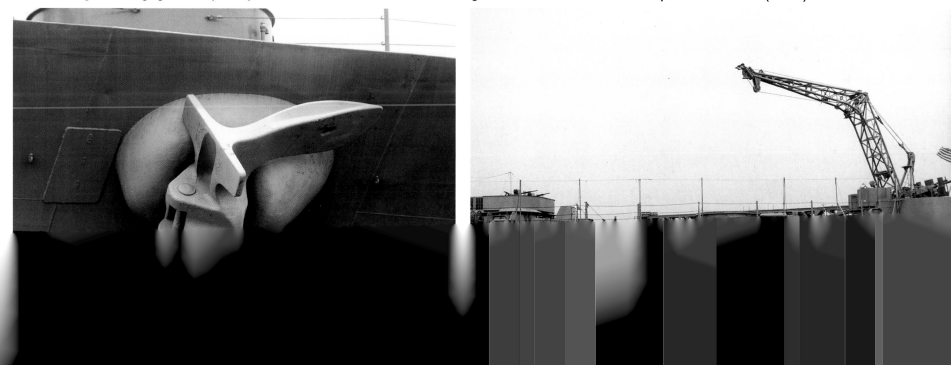

16-Inch Main Battery Turret

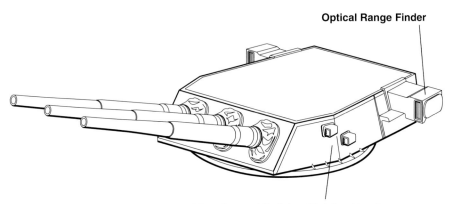

Optical Range Finder

Elevation and Training Sighting Hoods

16-Inch Turret Plan

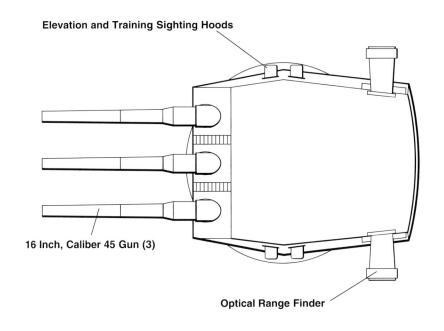

Elevation and Training Sighting Hoods

16 Inch, Caliber 45 Gun (3)

Optical Range Finder

The huge 16-inch guns of the *ALABAMA* now stand as a silent memorial to the men who fought and died during World War II. Each turret weighs 1500 tons — about the same as a World War II US Destroyer Escort's displacement. (Author)

(Above) The 16-inch guns of the *ALABAMA*'s forward turrets fire at targets on Saipan in 1944. The 16-inch diameter projectiles weighed 2700 pounds and had a range of over 20 miles. The guns could fire armor piercing (AP) shells against other ships or high explosive (HE) rounds against land targets. (Real War Photos)

(Above Right) Crewmen clean the snow off the *ALABAMA*'s deck during her Atlantic shake-down cruise in the winter of 1942-43. The cold and gray Atlantic would soon give way to the warmer climes of the South Pacific — and the Imperial Japanese Navy.

(Right) A crewman cleans snow off the 'bloomers' on the center 16-inch gun of Turret Two. The bloomers provided a seal to keep sea and rainwater out of the turret interior. Additionally, the bloomers were flexible, moving with the recoil of the guns when they were fired. (Elsilrac)

When the main battery was fired, the open 20mm anti-aircraft mounts on the forecastle were evacuated to prevent blast and concussion related injuries to the guns' crews. (Author)

The forward turrets contained three 16-inch/45 caliber Mark 45 naval guns. Each turret is 53 feet long, 40 feet wide, and weighs approximately 1437 long tons. (Author)

Turret Two sits on top of a raised armored barbette. The turret sides have 9.5 inches of armor, while the roof plates are fabricated from 7.25-inch armor plate. A quad 40mm anti-aircraft mount is placed aft on the turret roof. (Author)

Turret One is situated on the forward deck and sits on an armored barbette that extends below the main deck deep into the ship's interior. The turret is faced with 18-inch armor plate. (Author)

(Above) Each of the main battery turrets had a stereo-scopic optical range finder built into the after portion of the turret. The range finder was used during periods of ideal light or as a backup in the event the radar gun directors were inoperative. The optics provided the gunners with visual ranging to the target and were protected by armored hoods. This is the port rangefinder hood on Turret Three (the aft turret). (Author)

(Below) Turret Three was mounted on the quarter deck. Bronze plaques attached to the turret side trace the ALABAMA's wartime career. The main deck was made primarily from teak wood with other sections being made from steel. During her wartime service, the ALABAMA's decks were painted Deck Blue to blend into the sea. (Carol Adcock)

(Above) The number three turret rangefinder's position was located in the extreme rear section of the turret. The operator sat on a metal tractor type seat and sighted the guns through the binocular viewfinder. (Author)

Gunners in number one turret move a 16-inch projectile onto a hoist during the *ALABAMA*'s shakedown cruise. This round is a practice projectile, but it has the same size and weight of a live round. (Elsilrac)

A gunner's mate rams a 16-inch projectile into the breech of a gun in the number one turret. (Elsilrac)

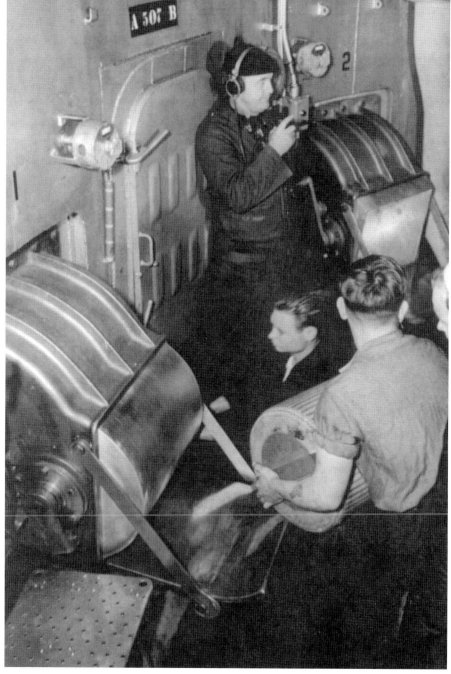

Additional powder bags roll out of the magazine in the barbette under Turret One. The powder bags were then hoisted into the turret. (Elsilrac)

Silk covered powder bags are rammed into the breech. This was a delicate operation requiring patience and skill. Gun elevation, and occasionally the number of powder bags, was used to vary the range of the main guns. (Real War Photos)

The five port side 5-inch mounts are staggered on deck levels 01 and 02. They were designated mounts 2,4,6,8 and 10 fore (at left) to aft. Staggering the mounts optimized the turrets' fields of fire while still allowing a compact arrangement. (Author)

The *ALABAMA* was equipped with twenty 5-inch/38 caliber Mark 32, Mod 12 dual purpose mounts in 10 fully enclosed turrets. Five mounts were placed to port and five were placed to starboard. This is the number five starboard side mount. (Author)

The enclosed 5-inch mounts had .75 inches of armor to protect the gun crew from small shells and shell splinters. Each mount weighs approximately 122,000 pounds — more than a US WW II PT Boat. (Author)

The 5-inch gun fired a 54-pound projectile that could be used against both air and ground targets depending on the type of round selected. The weapon fired both high explosive (HE) and armor piercing (AP) rounds. Additionally, the rounds could be fitted with contact or delayed action fuses. Proximity fuses were used against aircraft. Proximity fuses detonated the round when it passed within a specific distance of an aircraft. (Author)

The port side 5-inch mounts are on deck levels 01 and 02. The 5-inch guns were controlled by a Mark 37 Gun Director located on deck level 05. The small projections on the turrets' sides are secondary optical directors. All of the 16-inch, 5-inch, and 40mm weapons were equipped with a secondary optical aiming system in the event of loss or damage to the main gun directors. (Author)

The Mark 37 Gun Director was located on deck level 05 just above the numbers three and five 5-inch gun turrets. The director, which resembled a weaponless gun turret, used radar to determine range and bearing to the target. The *ALABAMA* possessed four Mk 37 Directors — one forward, one aft, and one each to port and starboard. (Author)

The number two portside 5-inch gun mount is seen from deck level 04. A quad 40mm anti-aircraft mount is located just below on deck level 01. (Author)

The 5-inch gun crews were provided with a pair of practice loading machines on the port side deck level 02 to increase their speed at loading the guns. (Author)

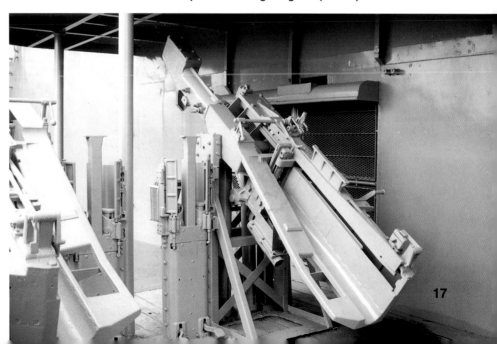

Dual 5-Inch/38 Caliber Turret

Plan View

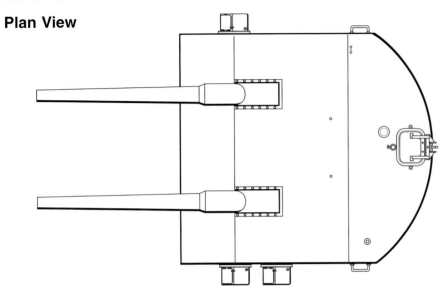

A 40mm quadruple (quad) anti-aircraft gun crew prepares to engage 'enemy' aircraft during a practice run in the Atlantic in 1943. The quad 40mm mount required a crew of 11. (Real War Photos)

A gun crew from the *ALABAMA*'s 10th Division loads rounds into their 40mm guns. The weapon was fed using four round clips locked into the top of the breech. The 40mm Bofors guns were designed in Sweden, and built in the US under license. (Real War Photos)

Port Profile

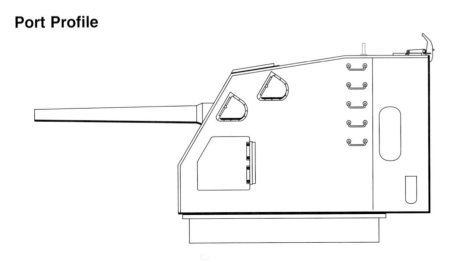

Quad 40mm Bofors Anti-Aircraft Mount

Without Shield

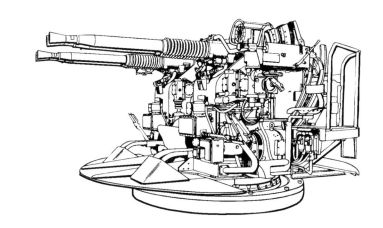

The 40mm quad anti-aircraft mount used a power traverse and elevation system, but could also be trained by hand in the event of power failures. The gun crew was protected from bomb and shell splinters by a Mark 3 gun shield. (Author)

One splinter shield moved with the gun. The entire mount was surrounded by a circular tub which also provided some protection against shell and bomb splinters. (Author)

With Shield

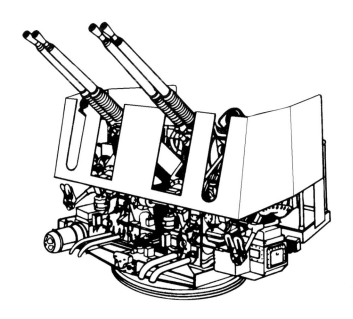

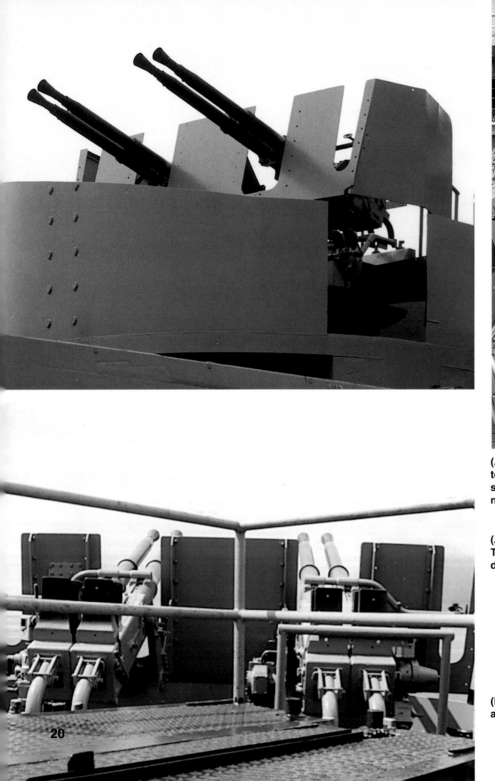

(Above) This port side 40mm mount has lag meters for the pointer and aimer mounted next to the seats. The handwheels provided manual elevation (left) and traverse (right). The four sets of brackets on the top of the gun breeches each held a four round clip of 40mm ammunition. (Author)

(Above Left) Quad 40mm mounts were also mounted on the roofs of Turrets Two and Three. The 40mm mounts replaced the originally fitted 20mm weapons. The 40mm mount was directed to a target by a Mark 52 Gun Director. (Author)

(Left) Two quad 40mm mounts placed on the stern to port and starboard provided additional protection from enemy aircraft attacking from the rear. (Author)

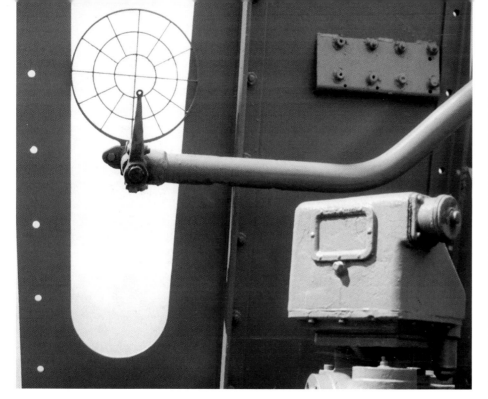

(Above) Both the pointer and aimer were provided with open ring-and-bead sights. The pointer's lag meter is visible at right. (Author)

(Above Right) The trainer's position was on the right side of the 40mm mount. The trainer's lag meter is mounted on the trainer's gearbox. The manual traverse handwheel is missing. (Author)

(Right) This gun's crew was protected by a circular, fixed Mk 3 shield around the base of the 40mm quad mount. Another shield is placed directly in front of the gun crew. This shield, which traverses with the guns, is missing its side flaps. Most shipboard 40mm weapons were water-cooled to prevent overheating during periods of intense action. (Author)

21

(Above) The *ALABAMA* carried 12 quad 40mm mounts — all placed to provide overlapping coverage against enemy air attack. This mount is on Deck Level 01. (Author)

(Above Left) The Number Three main battery turret mounted a quad 40mm antiaircraft weapon on the turret roof. These guns featured a wrap-around shield that moved with the cannons. A curtain of 40mm AA fire was the preferred method of dealing with close kamikaze attacks. The quad 40mm weapons' high rate of fire and powerful shell were highly effective against lightly built Japanese aircraft — much more so than the lighter, but faster firing 20mm Oerlikon weapons. (Author)

(Left) Four round clips were placed into the top of the breeches by the loaders. Each gun fired at a rate of up to 160 rounds per minute to a maximum range of 11,000 yards at 42° elevation. Expended cartridge cases were ejected out the rear of the breech and downward via the curved chutes. (Author)

(Above) The guns on the quad 40mm mount could elevate from -15˚ to +90˚. Both pairs of guns elevated as a single unit, but could be disengaged from each other in the event of damage to one pair. (Author)

(Below) The quad 40mm mounts worked in concert with the 5-inch/38 caliber dual purpose guns to provide a dense, multi-layered curtain of anti-aircraft fire. These are the port side weapons as viewed from the *ALABAMA*'s quarterdeck. (Carol Adcock)

(Above) A seagull is caught in the sight of this 40mm mount. Many years ago, it could just as easily been a Japanese Zero bent on crashing into the ship. (Author)

(Above) The gunner braced his shoulders against the curved pads and gripped the handle bars to elevate and traverse the weapon. The 20mm gun had a rate of fire of 450 rounds per minute. (Author)

(Above Left) The forward main deck was covered with several single and twin-barreled 20mm anti-aircraft gun mounts. The Oerlikon 20mm guns were designed in Switzerland and built in the US under license. The weapon was also used on aircraft. On board ship, the 20mm weapons were widely regarded as a last ditch, close-in defense weapon against incoming aircraft. (Author)

(Left) Single and twin barrel 20mm anti-aircraft weapons were mounted on the forecastle (pronounced foc'sle in USN parlance) deck. Both mounts were fed from 60 round drum magazines. (Author)

(Above) Three Mk 10 dual 20mm mounts were placed on the port side main deck. These weapons were not manned when the main battery 16-inch guns were in use due to blast effects on the gun crews. By 1945 the *ALABAMA* was armed with 56 20mm anti-aircraft weapons in both single and dual mounts. (Carol Adcock)

(Right) The gun sights are missing on this weapon. Both ring-and-bead and Mk 14 electric sights could be used. The one half-inch thick gun shield was sufficient to stop rifle caliber bullets fired from a strafing aircraft or light splinters from exploding shells — beyond that, the gunner and his loaders were largely unprotected. Two 60-round 20mm ammunition drums are mounted on top of the breeches. The left shoulder rest has been bent out of shape. (Author)

These quarterdeck 20mm guns are mounted between the 16-inch turret and a quad 40mm mount. The gun shield traverses with the gun, but does not elevate, hence the cutout at the top of the shield. The guns could elevate from -15° to +90°. (Author)

A typical single 20mm Mk 10 mount with a Mk 4 gun shield is equipped with a Mk 4 ring-and-bead sight. The weapon had a range of approximately 4800 yards. The 60-round ammunition drum could be emptied in approximately eight seconds. A loader would be standing by, instantly ready to pull the empty drum off the breech and snap another into place. (Author)

20mm Mk 10 Single Mount

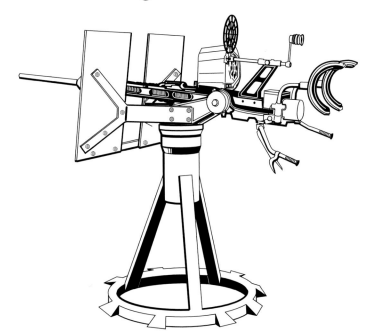

Gunsight Mk 4 (Open)

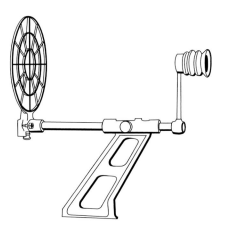

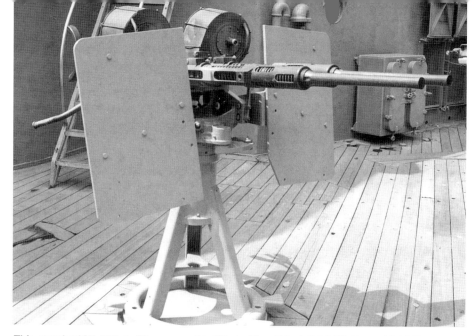

This standard Mk 20 twin 20mm mount is fitted with a .5-inch thick Mk 7 gunshield. The 20mm weapons were the last close-in defense weapon against incoming enemy aircraft. (Author)

These 20mm mounts are equipped with the Mk 14 electric gunsight. This was the standard gun sight for all 20mm and 40mm mounts by the end of World War II. (Author)

Gunsight Mk 10 (Electric)

20mm Mk 20 Dual Mount

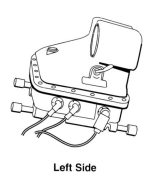

Left Side

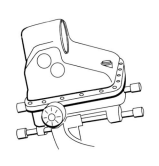

Right Side

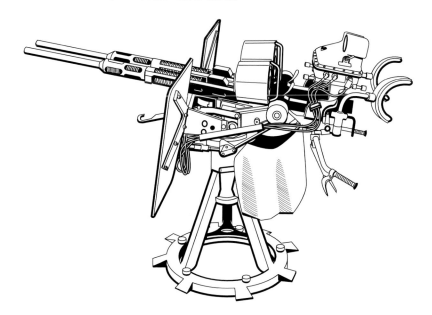

(Above) Many 20mm mounts, where space allowed, were provided with extra shielding to protect the gun crews. Owing to Japanese Kamikaze attacks, US Navy ships were covered with light and medium anti-aircraft weapons. Quad 40mm and twin 5-inch mounts are also visible. (Author)

(Above Left) These 20mm mounts are placed atop the fantail vent housings. The gun tub provided additional splinter protection. The *ALABAMA* and her sister ships, the *SOUTH DAKOTA*, *MASSACHUSETTS*, and *INDIANA* often functioned as floating anti-aircraft batteries to protect other US Navy ships and US Marine amphibious vessels from enemy air attack. (Author)

(Left) Twenty millimeter Oerlikon anti-aircraft mounts were placed on three different deck levels on both the port and starboard sides of the ship. (Author)

(Above) These 20mm weapons were placed in 'gun galleries' on both the port and starboard sides of the quarterdeck. These starboard side mounts are placed behind a splinter shield. The gun barrel recoil springs are visible through the slots in the barrel sleeve. (Carol Adcock)

This 20mm weapon, mounted on the fantail vent housing, lacks its shoulder supports and gun sights. Single barrel 20mm weapons used a smaller handle bar grip. The trigger was mounted on the left handgrip. The mount allowed the weapon to be traversed in a 360˚ circle, however many mounts were equipped with gun stops to keep overzealous gunners from accidentally firing into their own ship. (Author)

Crews from the 10th Division relax at the ready in their triple berthing in 1943. Their helmets and life vests were close at hand. The berths could be folded up against the bulkhead when not in use. (Real War Photos)

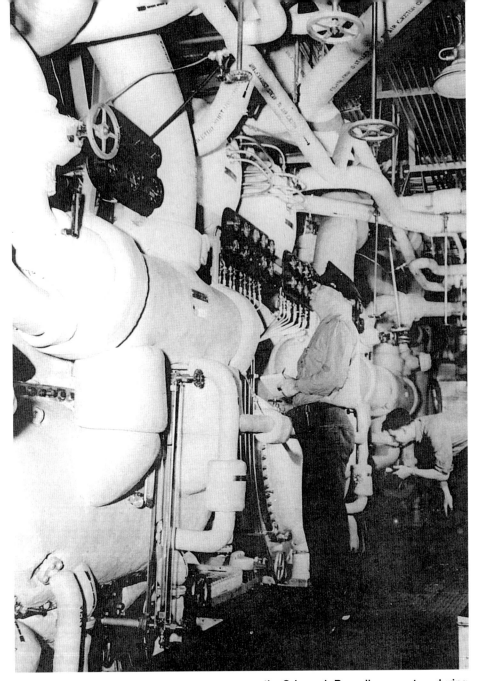

The Chief Boilertender checks pressure gauges on the Griscomb-Russell evaporators during a shakedown cruise in early 1943. Four sets of boilers and engines propelled the *ALABAMA* up to a speed of 28 knots (31.6 mph). One knot equals 1.13 mph. (Elsilrac)

The almost complete USS *ALABAMA* is fitted out at Norfolk Navy Yard in this wartime painting from 1942. The forward section of the bridge has yet to be built around the armored conning tower. The Measure 12 camouflage scheme has been applied to the hull. (Elsilrac)

The *ALABAMA's* superstructure is covered with guns, gun directors, and radars from the main deck to deck level 08. Added to the superstructure are communications antennas, hose reels, ammunition and equipment lockers, and vents. Radar antennas are placed high on both fore and main masts to increase their coverage. All of the defensive equipment is located in order to provide as much overlapping coverage as possible in a 360° circle around the ship.

Under normal steaming conditions the ship was conned from the open bridge. In combat conditions the ship was controlled from the armored conning tower, an oval shaped citadel designed to be impervious to fire from other battleships. The modified ship navigating bridge was added during an overhaul in 1944. (Author)

Direct vision slots were cut into the conning tower armor. The spike in the view slit is a sight to provide a steering reference for the helmsman. (Author)

Battle Ribbons, a scoreboard of Japanese aircraft shot down, and a record of Japanese held island bombardments are placed on the bridge area to both port and starboard. The ALABAMA earned the American Service Medal, European-African Service Medal, Asiatic Pacific Campaign Medal with 9 Battlestars, Philippine Republic Presidential Unit Citation, Philippine Liberation Medal, World War Two Victory Medal and the Navy Occupation Service Medal. (Bill Tunnel)

(Above) The USS *ALABAMA* is barely underway in the relatively calm waters of Chesapeake Bay on 30 November 1942. The camouflage pattern is a modified Measure 12 scheme of Ocean Gray and Navy Blue. (Floating Drydock)

(Below) The *ALABAMA* is viewed from the starboard quarter on 30 November 1942. The compact superstructure and single funnel were easily recognized on the *SOUTH DAKOTA* class battleships. (Floating Drydock)

34

The *ALABAMA* was fitted with two bridge configurations during her wartime career. The first, fitted during her construction, was an open style bridge. Later, the *ALABAMA* received a closed version to protect the bridge crew from the elements. While the shield- ing could protect the bridge crew from machine gun fire and light shell splinters, it was by no means able to stop incoming large caliber shells. The late style bridge with the square windows was also fitted to many late war destroyers and cruisers.

Bridge Configuration - 1942

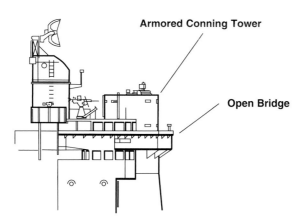

Armored Conning Tower

Open Bridge

Bridge Configuration - 1945

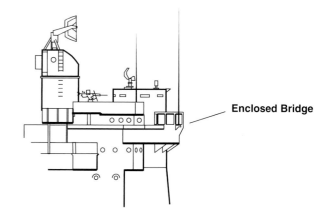

Enclosed Bridge

The single gas stack was incorporated into the after part of the ship's superstructure. The larger *IOWA* class battleships had a similar arrangement, but added a second funnel further aft. (Author)

The *ALABAMA* was fitted with a variety of search and signal lights. This search light on the port side lacks the focusing lens used to narrow and intensify the light beam. Searchlights were capable of throwing a concentrated beam of light several miles and illuminating targets at night. (Author)

(Below) Cable reels were mounted at various points around the deck. The metal cable could be used for any task requiring more strength than rope. (Author)

(Above) The quarterdeck housed several anti-aircraft gun galleries, vents, access ports, cable and hose reels, and equipment lockers. The area around Turret Three was kept relatively clear to allow the turret room to traverse and fire. (Carol Adcock)

(Below) Roller chocks were fitted to both the port and starboard sides. The rounded surfaces and vertical rollers allowed heavy cables and mooring lines to pass over the side of the ship without snagging on the hull or deck equipment. (Author)

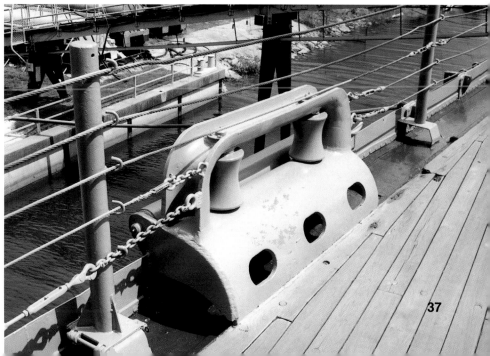

The *ALABAMA* rides at anchor in late 1942. She is equipped with the early style bridge configuration which consisted of an open platform wrapped around the armored conning tower. The Measure 12 Ocean Gray and Navy Blue splotched camouflage scheme was changed to a Measure 22 Haze Gray and Navy Blue graded scheme when *ALABAMA* began combat operations in the Atlantic in 1943.

(Above) The *ALABAMA*, like most battleships, was built in layers. The size of the layers grew smaller as they became higher. This allowed an unobstructed field of fire for the guns and an unobstructed field of view for the gun directors and radars. Both the bridge and armored conning tower were given a clear field of view over the main battery turrets forward and to port and starboard to improve ship handling.

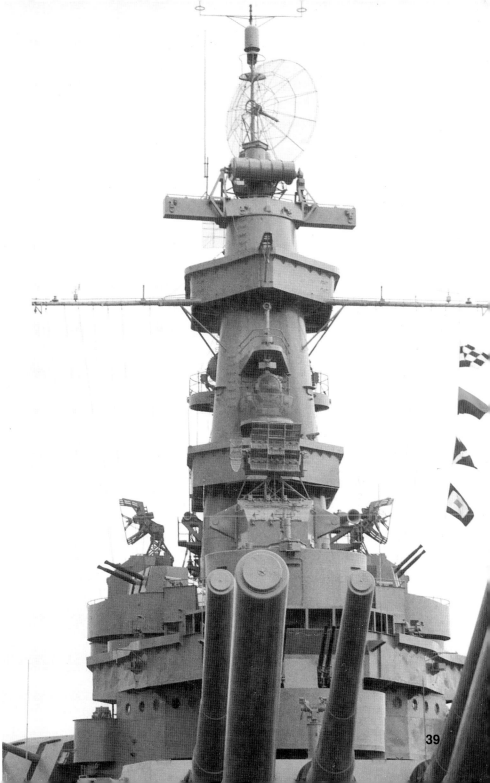

(Right) The towering superstructure of the *ALABAMA* was covered with a variety of platforms and catwalks to provide mounting points for gun directors, search and signal lights, yardarms, and antennas. The Mk 38 main battery gun director and the Mk 8 radar were placed atop the tower — the highest part of the superstructure — where it could see over the horizon.

39

A windlass (a large drum shaped winch) hauled the anchor up from the water. Notches in the windlass drum engaged the links of the chain — much like a drive sprocket on a bicycle. The windlass could be braked using the horizontal wheel at right. The starboard windlass is not fitted. (Author)

Large hooks were attached to deck projections between the anchor chains to prevent unwanted movement. Additional steel plating was added to the deck under the chains to prevent damage. The hatches by the windlass lead to the crew berthing. (Author)

Several tons of anchor and anchor chain were required to hold the *ALABAMA* in place. The anchor chains ran aft across the open foredeck to the windlass — a large motorized winch — and then below deck to the chain locker. Mud and seaweed were usually hosed off the anchor and chains when they were hauled up from the seabed.

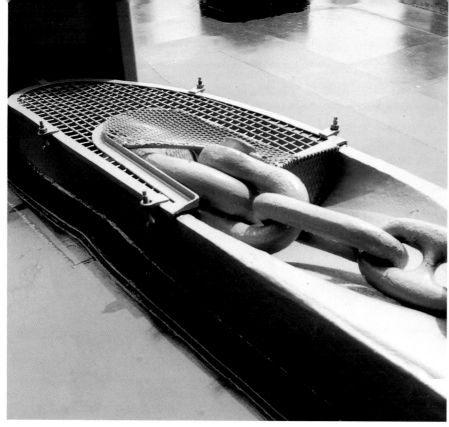

The rounded sides and gentle bends in the hawsepipe prevented the links of the anchor chain from snagging on the deck when it was brought up from the seabed. The hawsepipes have been fitted with additional screening to prevent tourists from falling into the opening. (Author)

Anchor System Specifications

Anchor Weight: 25,000 lbs (12.5 Tons)
Anchor Chain Link Weight: 105 lbs
Anchor Chain Length: 170 Fathoms*

*One fathom equals six feet; total chain length is 1020 feet.

The anchor chain ran from the chain locker below deck, across the fore deck, and into the hawsepipe. The hawsepipe was a chute which provided the heavy anchor chain a free run from the water to the deck. (Author)

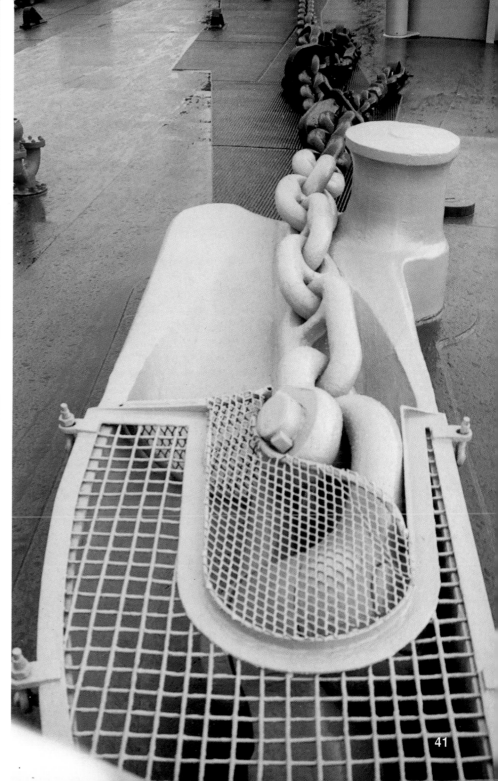

The *ALABAMA* drops anchor on a cold, wet day in late 1942. Two crewmen on anchor detail are operating the starboard windlass brake. The cover has been taken off the chute leading to the chain locker. (Real War Photos)

Paravane Operations

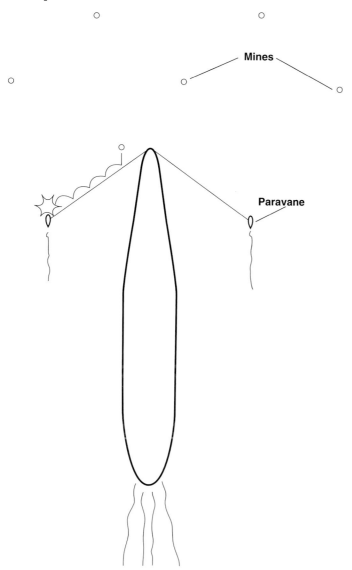

Mines

Paravane

Crewmen aboard a small minecraft prepare to launch a paravane. The paravane was trailed in the water by cables and designed to fend off mines and cut mine cables. The floating mine could then be detonated by gunfire. Paravanes on the *ALABAMA* were normally stowed to port and starboard on the fore deck behind the sheerwater. The sheerwater was a large V-shaped deflector designed to channel water off the foredeck and over the sides of the ship. (Elsilrac)

(Below) The Mk 38 director was used to direct the 16-inch guns. The guns could be corrected by tracking the shell splashes of previously fired rounds. The director was also equipped with a stereoscopic range finder in the large side arms for visual target acquisition and gun laying. (Author)

(Above) US Navy ships were equipped with various gun directors, both optical and radar. From left to right are the Mk 38 gun director with Mk 8 radar (main battery), Mk 52 gun director (40mm), and Mk 37 gun director with Mk 22 and Mk 12 radar (secondary battery). (Carol Adcock)

(Below) The Mk 8 radar was mounted on the roof of the Mk 38 director. The director was lightly armored to provide some splinter protection for the crew. (Author)

Gun Director Mk 38 w/ Mk 8 Radar

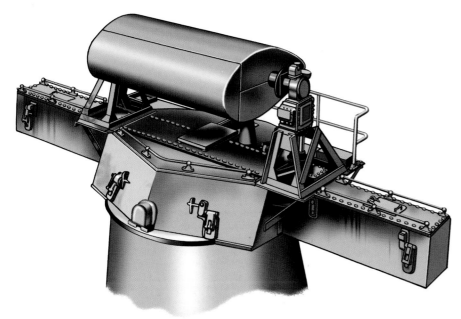

The Mk 38 gun director was equipped with a Mk 8 radar. The system was designed for use with the main battery 16-inch guns and provided target range, course, and speed to the fire control computers buried inside the superstructure. The forward facing rods of the Mk 8 radar were often enclosed within an environmental cover to protect the components from the weather. The stack to the left of the louvers is the exhaust for one of the two onboard auxiliary 200 kilowatt generators. (Author)

(Above) The *ALABAMA*, still wearing a Measure 12 camouflage scheme, cruises in Casco Bay, Maine in late 1942, just prior to her shakedown in the Atlantic. The battleship has her original open style bridge and has not yet received her full complement of 40mm AA weapons. (Elsilrac)

(Below) The *ALABAMA* wore a new camouflage scheme known as Measure 22 on 7 February 1943. The scheme consisted of Navy Blue on the hull up to the lowest point of the sheer and Haze Gray on all vertical surfaces above the sheer (the sheer was where the main deck started to curve upwards at the bow and stern.) The *ALABAMA* would soon sail through the Panama Canal and into the Pacific Theater. (Floating Drydock)

The *ALABAMA* is anchored in the choppy waters of Chesapeake Bay in February of 1943. Both anchors were normally used when anchoring in relatively open waters. This was often the case in the Pacific where open water anchorages in large lagoons were commonplace. Turret One is trained to starboard. (Floating Drydock)

The broad beamed hull and compact superstructure of the *ALABAMA* are emphasized while the battleship is anchored in Chesapeake Bay in February of 1943. The guns of turret three are elevated to their maximum of +45°. (Floating Drydock)

The after gun directors were mounted on the ship's centerline and could direct fire aft and to port and starboard. The middle director is a Mk 52 Gun Director used to lay the 40mm Bofors anti-aircraft guns. (Author)

The ALABAMA carried two Mk 38 gun directors with Mk 8 radars — one forward at the highest point of the superstructure and this one aft of the funnel. (Author)

The upper section of the tower contained a platform and mounts for the yardarms while a Mk 38 gun director and Mk 8 radar were mounted on the top. The director traversed to port and starboard and provided both a radar and optical view of a target for the main battery. (Author)

Two masts were mounted on the ALABAMA — one attached to the rear of the tower and one deck mounted behind the single funnel. Both masts were used to mount additional radar and communications antennas. (Author)

Left to right are the Mk 52 40mm gun director and range-only radar, a Mk 37 gun director with Mk 12 and 22 radars for the 5-inch guns, and the Number Three 16-inch turret mounted quad 40mm guns. (Author)

Gun Director
Mk 37, 1944-1945

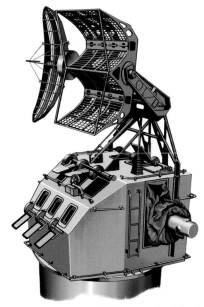

The Mk 37 5-inch gun director bore a superficial resemblance to the 5-inch gun turrets. The large radar is a Mk 12 ranging and tracking radar, while the smaller elliptical radar antenna is a Mk 22 height finding radar. The Mk 37 gun director was employed against both surface and air targets. (Author)

(Above) The *ALABAMA* buries her bow in heavy Atlantic seas on 4 March 1943. She does not yet have the new navigation bridge with the square windows. (Real War Photos)

(Below) The *ALABAMA* speeds alongside the light carrier USS *MONTERREY* (CVL-26) while in the Pacific in January of 1944. The *ALABAMA* is now camouflaged in Measure 21 — an overall Navy Blue scheme. (Elsilrac)

(Above) A bomb lands in the water abreast of the *ALABAMA*'s Number Two turret off of Saipan on 19 June 1944. The *ALABAMA* came under air attack several times during WW II, but never received damage from enemy action. (Real War Photos)

(Right) Crewmen of the barely underway *ALABAMA* crowd her sun drenched deck on 20 August 1943. The teak wood and steel decks were painted Deck Blue to help the ship blend into the sea. (Elsilrac)

51

(Above) The backside of the Mk 12 Mod 4 and elliptical MK 22 Mod 0 radars reveals their mounting structure. The Mk 12 and 22 radars were used for the 5-inch guns. (Author)

(Left) The after Mk 37 gun director was mounted on the *ALABAMA*'s centerline. Four Mk 37 directors were used for the 10 dual 5-inch mounts. The Number Three main battery turret range finder is in the foreground. (Author)

(Above) The elliptical Mk 22 radar (at right) was specifically designed to find the altitude of an aerial target and was particularly useful at detecting low altitude targets. (Author)

(Right) The Mk 12 radar was used for ranging and bearing calculations by the fire control computer. The use of four directors allowed a measure of redundancy — the loss or damage of one director did not necessarily mean the loss of coverage in any one direction. (Author)

(Above) The *ALABAMA* was anchored in Puget Sound, Washington on 15 March 1945. The battleship is once again wearing the Measure 22 camouflage scheme — the same scheme she wore in 1943. A new navigating bridge (with square windows) has been added to the superstructure. (Floating Drydock)

(Below) The refitted USS *ALABAMA* was anchored in Puget Sound, Washington before leaving for the less friendly waters of the western Pacific. The forward guns are locked into different elevations. The guns of Turrets One and Three could be elevated from -2° to +45°, while the guns of Turret Two could be elevated from 0° to +45°. (Floating Drydock)

(Above) The *ALABAMA* throws up a curtain of 20mm, 40mm, and 5-inch anti-aircraft fire off Saipan in 1944. The battleship's combined anti-aircraft batteries could put over 25,000 rounds into the air per minute. (Real War Photos)

(Below) An aircraft from the USS *BUNKER HILL* (CV-17) photographed the *ALABAMA* turning hard to starboard on 24 January 1944. Turret Three is trained to starboard. (Real War Photos)

(Above) The radar antennae of the after centerline Mk 37 gun director loom above one of the port side 40mm gun mounts. (Author)

(Above Left) Silent guns and directors continue to scan the sky while the *ALABAMA* rests at Battleship Memorial Park. One of the *ALABAMA*'s bronze colored, five- bladed outboard propellers rests in the foreground. The *ALABAMA* employed four propellers under her stern. The four-bladed propellers on the inboard shafts were 17 feet, 6 inches in diameter, while the five-bladed propellers on the outboard shafts were larger by 2.5 inches. At full power the *ALABAMA* could make up to 28 knots — or 31.6 mph.

(Left) Mk 37 Gun Directors were also mounted to port and starboard. This is the starboard Mk 37 gun director. Many components mounted to the upper superstructure — such as the platform at upper right — had lightening holes in them to reduce top weight. (Author)

(Above) The integration of the forward superstructure tower and the stack into a single unit allowed both elements to share some of the upper armor protection. This arrangement was repeated on the larger *IOWA*-class battleships, although the *IOWAs*' increased length allowed the use of a second funnel. (Author)

(Above Right) The Mk 37 Gun Director had a crew of six to seven men, all engaged in using radar, optics, or communications systems. (Author)

(Right) The Mk 12 radar had a range of approximately 45,000 yards against aircraft. The elliptical Mk 22 radar performance was similar. The Mk 22 radar was particularly useful against low flying aircraft. (Author)

(Above) The *ALABAMA* departs Hawaii for the U.S. west coast on 9 October 1945. The battleship is carrying Curtiss SC-1 Seahawk floatplanes on her fantail. Battleship and cruiser deployed floatplanes quickly became obsolete once helicopters began to see widespread service. (Elsilrac)

(Below) The *ALABAMA* was assigned to the US 3rd Fleet when she left Hawaii for the US coast in October of 1945. (Elsilrac)

The war is over and many of *ALABAMA*'s light and medium AA weapons have been covered with canvas to protect them from the elements. Curiously, there are few men on the deck. Perhaps there was now more time for spit-and-polish in the peacetime Navy. (Floating Drydock)

Both Vought OS2U Kingfisher floatplanes are missing in this photo taken in 1944. There was no provision for covered aircraft storage on the *SOUTH DAKOTA* class battleships. The Kingfishers were usually secured to the catapults where they had to take everything mother nature could throw at them. (Real War Photos)

Gun Director Mk 52 (40mm AA)

A circular SK-2 air search radar was mounted atop the mast fastened to the forward super-structure. The radar rotated through 360° and had a range of up to 80,000 yards against aircraft. The domed housing above the SK-2 covers an SU surface search radar. The larger domed housing adjacent to the SK-2 covers a TDY radar jammer. (Author)

The Mk 52 gun director was used to control the 40mm anti-aircraft guns. The Mk 52 director used a range-only radar. (Author)

(Above) The Mk 38 Gun Director atop the superstructure mounted an improved Mk 13 fire control radar in lieu of the earlier Mk 8 radar. The *ALABAMA* retained the Mk 38/Mk 8 combination on the after main battery fire control director. The large rectangular antenna on the main mast is an SR air search radar. The smaller parabolic dish on the stub mast is an SG surface search radar. (Author)

(Right) By the last year of WW II, US Navy ships were outfitted with several kinds of air and surface search radars and fire control radars. There was sometimes great difficulty in finding a place to put all the radar antennas. US radar technology at this stage of the war far outstripped that of Germany or Japan. (Author)

(Port) The *ALABAMA* moves through the Gaillard Cut in the Panama Canal with tugs at the bow, stern, and at tow. The tugs at the bow and stern prevent the unpowered battleship from drifting too far left or right within the confines of the Canal. The ship lacks her AA weapons as well as both catapults. (Elsilrac)

(Below) The *ALABAMA* is towed through the Panama Canal in 1964. The ship's propellers have been removed and stored on the foc'sle. This was the longest and most expensive tow in history and cost over one million dollars — most of the funds being raised by Alabama school children. (Elsilrac)

(Starboard) The *ALABAMA* is moored in a deep channel at Battleship Park, Mobile, Alabama. Her paint finish is now Measure 27, an overall pale gray scheme used on current US Navy vessels. The large white hull number with the black shadow is also a modern addition. (Elsilrac)

(Below) The Union Jack, a blue flag with 48 white stars, flutters from the jack staff mounted on the *ALABAMA*'s prow. *ALABAMA* has her original tower and mast mounted antenna fit. Compare this fit with the later 1945 fit pictured at right. The rapid increases in technology driven by the war situation often meant new equipment was fitted every time the battleship entered a major port or repair facility.

Storm clouds gather over the *ALABAMA*'s silent guns. The 16-inch diameter gun muzzles are sealed with a tampion to prevent further corrosion. (Author)

The fantail is covered with steel decking, while further forward the quarterdeck is covered with the original natural teak wood. During *ALABAMA*'s WW II service, both surfaces were painted overall Deck Blue. (Author)

A Kingfisher is about to be launched from the starboard catapult on the *ALABAMA* in 1943. The Kingfishers were assigned to Battleship Division Nine (VO-9). The Kingfishers were stored in the open since *ALABAMA* lacked hangar facilities. (Elsilrac)

(Below) The aircraft handling crane is capable of rotating through 360° in order to pick floatplanes out of the water and place them on the catapults. (Author)

(Above) The *ALABAMA* and her three sister ships were equipped with an aircraft handling crane mounted on the fantail. The US flag flies from the fantail when the ship is in port. At sea, the flag flies from the main mast. (Carol Adcock)

(Below) The aircraft handling crane was also used to handle the Captain's launch, whale boats, and various other heavy materials and supplies. (Author)

(Above) The two aircraft catapults were mounted on the quarterdeck between Turret Three and the aircraft handling crane. The catapults could pivot on a central turntable. When not in use the catapults were usually aligned with the edge of the ship's hull. The catapults were turned out to the ship's side when launching aircraft. The ship's course could be altered and the catapult angled to provide optimum takeoff conditions — into the wind — for the floatplanes. (Author)

(Right) The aircraft handling crane is raised in its normal upright and operating condition. The crane could be laid down flat on the deck in the event of adverse weather. In addition to aircraft, the crane also handled launches and brought supplies aboard. (Author)

(Above) The original aircraft catapults were removed before the ship arrived at the park. This catapult was salvaged from a cruiser about to be scrapped. It is generally similar to the catapults used on the *ALABAMA* during her wartime service. (Author)

(Left) The catapult was 68 feet long and could be trained to launch the floatplane in almost any direction off the side of the ship. (Author)

(Above) The catapult was powered by an explosive charge —similar to a 5-inch gun round, but without the projectile — and designed to launch an aircraft from 0 to 70 mph in approximately one second. (Author)

(Right) The *ALABAMA*'s Vought OS2U Kingfisher was a wreck found in Mexico and turned over to the Battleship Commission for restoration. The Kingfisher was displayed on the *ALABAMA*'s catapult until it was damaged in a storm. The aircraft was repaired and placed in a hanger on the grounds of the Battleship Memorial Park for security. Here the fuselage has been separated from the central float which is still mounted on the catapult behind the aircraft. (Author)

The Vought-OS2U-1 Kingfisher was a scout-observation aircraft that first went into US Navy fleet service in 1940 aboard the battleship *NORTH CAROLINA* (BB-55). The two-man crew consisted of a pilot and observer-gunner. (LTV Corp.)

The Kingfisher could be operated as a land-based aircraft by removing the floats and bolting on fixed landing gear. The Kingfisher became the standard US Navy shipboard floatplane and saw widespread service in both the Atlantic and Pacific Oceans. (USN)

The USS *ALABAMA* wore a two-color Measure 12 camouflage scheme consisting of gray and blue during 1942. This scheme was used during her sea trials and crew training. Her decks were stained Deck Blue to help her blend into the sea when observed from the air. The *ALABAMA* carried Deck Blue on her decks throughout the war.

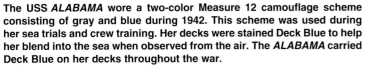

USS *ALABAMA*
Insignia

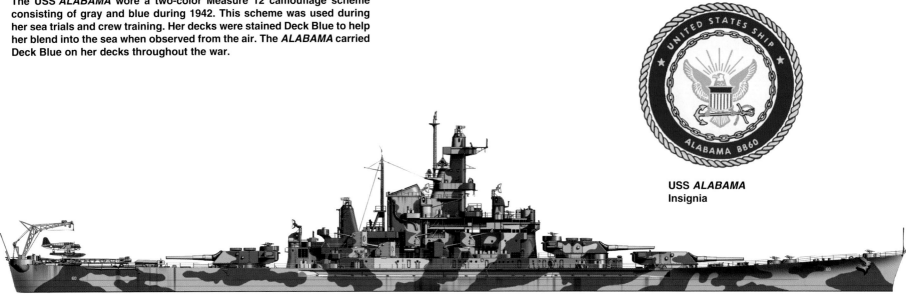

The Measure 12 scheme was different on the port side of the ship, but used the same colors. These camouflage schemes were designed to make the ship more difficult to see. The camouflage also broke up the ship's outline in order to confuse the ship's identity and inhibit an adversary's ability to accurately gauge her course and speed.

Arm Band worn by dockyard crews during the launching of the USS *ALABAMA*

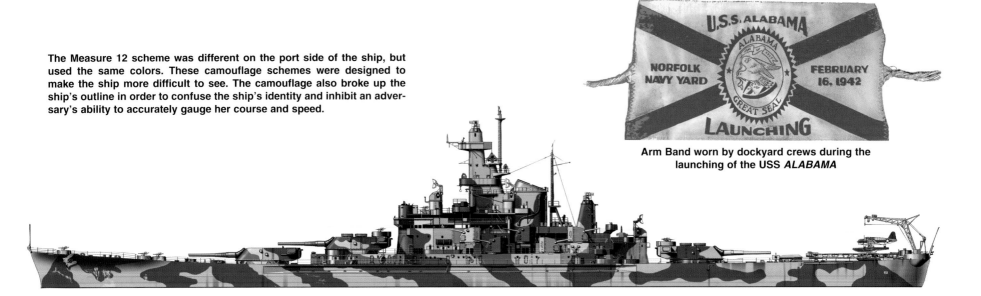

The *ALABAMA* wore an overall blue Measure 21 camouflage scheme during her initial operations in the Pacific in early 1944. During this period, the *ALABAMA* also began to receive upgraded radars and an increasing number of anti-aircraft weapons. The dark blue hull and superstructure, combined with the dark blue decks, allowed the battleship to blend into the sea when viewed from the air, but did tend to silhouette the ship against the horizon when viewed from the surface.

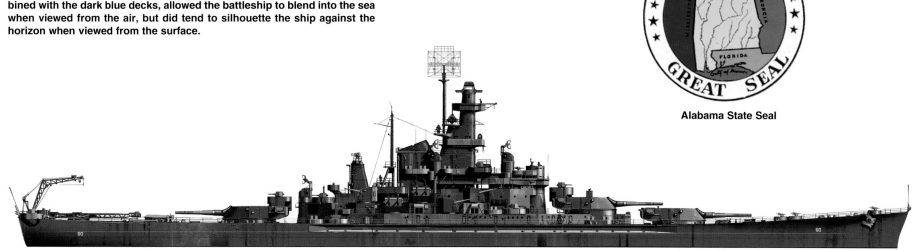

Alabama State Seal

The *ALABAMA* was repainted in the blue and gray Measure 22 camouflage scheme for her later operations in the Pacific. This scheme was also worn during the *ALABAMA*'s operations in the Atlantic in 1943. The Navy Blue hull blended into the sea, while the lighter grey paint on the superstructure kept the superstructure from standing out against the horizon. The *ALABAMA* also received newer radar equipment and additional anti-aircraft weapons to deal with the ever increasing threat of Japanese *kamikaze* attacks.

Alabama Coat of Arms

(Below) Vought OS2U-3s cruise off Biloxi, Mississippi during the summer of 1943. Kingfishers wore the standard US Navy scheme of Sea Blue, Intermediate Blue, and white. The floats are believed to be painted silver. The *ALABAMA* carried two Kingfishers on her fantail. (Scheel)

(Above) A Kingfisher, believed to be a Naval Aircraft Factory-built OS2N-1, is launched from the starboard catapult in late 1943. Smoke from the powder charge used to launch the floatplane billows up over the fantail. Kingfishers were used for spotting the effects of the ship's gunfire and in air-sea rescue missions. (Edo Corp.)

(Below) The Kingfisher reached flying speed by the time it reached the end of the catapult. Drooped ailerons, interconnected with the lowered flaps, provided additional lift. (Walter Turner via Thad Rudd)

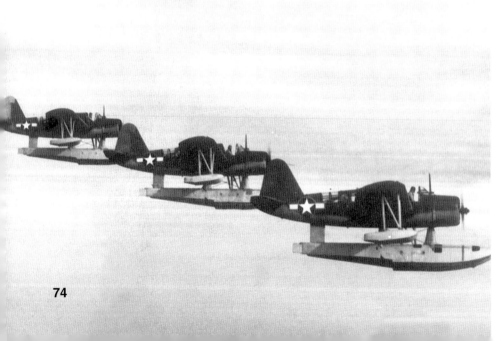

74

A Kingfisher is hauled aboard by the aircraft handling crane. The floatplane would land in the ship's smooth wake and taxi forward until a hook (barely visible below the center float) engaged a towing sled. The ship would tow the aircraft until the back seat crewman hooked the crane's hoist to the aircraft. This was not the easiest of jobs in rough weather and choppy water — that's why the enlisted man was tasked to do it...

After the war, the *ALABAMA* was repainted in an overall Measure 13 scheme. The battleship wore this scheme until she was decommissioned and mothballed in early 1947. The post-war period also saw the ship stripped of many of her no longer needed light anti-aircraft weaponry.

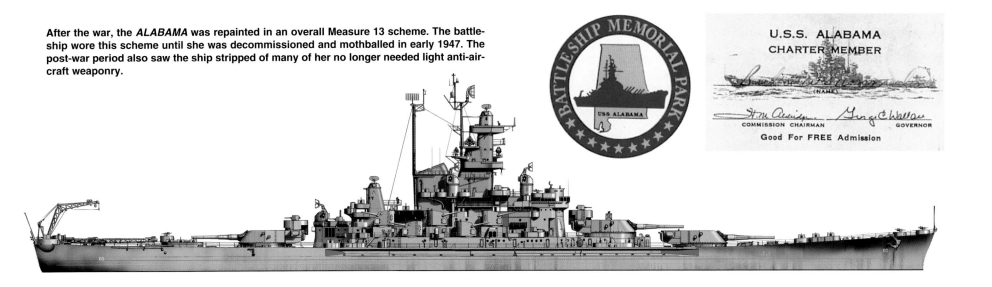

U.S.S. ALABAMA
CHARTER MEMBER

(NAME)

COMMISSION CHAIRMAN   GOVERNOR

Good For FREE Admission

The USS *ALABAMA* is now moored in Battleship Memorial Park in Mobile Bay, Alabama where she is visited by thousands of visitors every year. Getting the ship to her final resting place took several weeks and over a million dollars — most of the funds being raised by Alabama school children. Each contributor received a U.S.S. ALABAMA CHARTER MEMBER card.

The two-seat Vought OS2U Kingfisher was designed as a shipboard, catapult launched observation and scouting aircraft. The Kingfisher was widely used to spot the effects of the ship's gunfire and used radio to provide corrections to the guns' range and bearing. The *ALABAMA* carried two OS2U aircraft — both camouflaged in non-specular (flat) sea blue, intermediate blue, and white. This Kingfisher wears the US insignia with the red surround which was introduced in June of 1943 and replaced in August of 1943 by a blue bordered insignia.

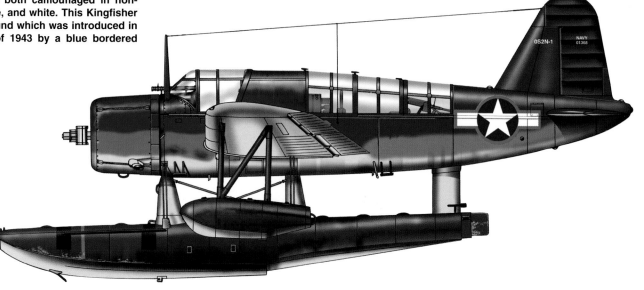

The single seat Curtiss SC-1 Seahawk was designed to replace the Kingfisher aboard US Navy battleships and cruisers. The SC-1 offered improved performance and had folding wings to facilitate shipboard stowage. Most of the Seahawks wore an overall dark glossy sea blue camouflage scheme. This SC-1 also carries the blue bordered US insignia introduced in August of 1943.

The single-seat Curtiss SC-1 Seahawk began to replace the Vought Kingfisher aboard US Navy battleships and cruisers in 1945. The SC-1 was powered by a 9-cylinder Wright R-1820 radial engine driving a four bladed propeller. The engine was also used on the Boeing B-17 Flying Fortress and the US Navy's own FM-2 Wildcat.

(Below) The Seahawk was equipped with folding wings which greatly eased shipboard stowage. Early SC-1s wore the USN tricolor scheme of Sea Blue, Intermediate Blue, and white. Later Seahawks were painted overall Sea Blue. (Morely)

(Above) The Seahawk was a single seat scout-observation aircraft that offered increased performance over all previous US Navy shipboard float aircraft. The Seahawks aboard the *ALABAMA* were assigned to Battleship Division Eight (VO-8). This SC-1 has engaged the rope sled and is about to be brought aboard. (Real War Photos)

(Below) The Seahawk could be operated as a land-based aircraft by removing the floats and adding bolt-on landing gear — a capability shared with the OS2U Kingfisher. The war ended before the SC-1 could be procured in substantial numbers. (Morley)

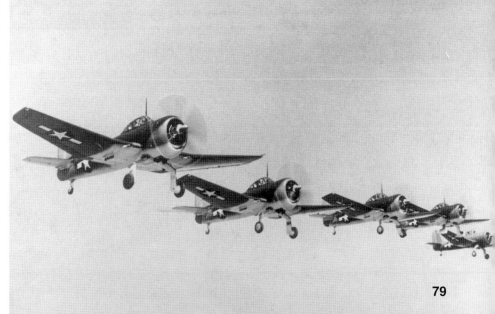

Visit the
USS ALABAMA
at
Battleship Memorial Park

2703 Battleship Parkway (Highway 90/98), Mobile, Alabama. Exits 27 or 30 off Interstate 10
Telephone (334) 433-2703
Open 8:00 AM daily (except Christmas)
See over 20 military aircraft and ten military vehicles from World War Two to the present.
Visit the restaurant, snack bar, theater, and flight simulator.

The tour includes the

USS DRUM

a World War Two Gato class submarine with 13 war patrols and 15 enemy ships to her credit.